WISE QUOTES: BENJAMIN FRANKLIN

(112 BENJAMIN FRANKLIN QUOTES)

Rowan Stevens

A brother may not be a friend, but a friend will always be a brother.

A fat kitchen makes a lean will.

A great talker may be no fool, but he is one that relies on him.

A learned blockhead is a greater blockhead than an ignorant one.

A man of words and not of deeds, is like a garden full of weeds.

A new truth is a truth, an old error is an error.

A penny saved is a penny earned.

After all, wedlock is the natural state of man. A bachelor is not a complete human being. He is like the odd half of a pair of scissors, which has not yet found its fellow, and therefore is not even half so useful as they might be together.

An old young man will be a young old man.

An ounce of prevention is worth a pound of cure.

Be not sick too late, nor well too soon.

Be studious in your profession, and you will be learned. Be industrious and frugal and you will be rich. Be sober and temperate and you will be healthy. Be in general virtuous and you will be happy.

Beware of little expenses. A small leak will sink a great ship.

By failing to prepare, you are preparing to fail.

By the collision of different sentiments, sparks of truth are struck out, and political light is obtained. The different factions, which at present divide us, aim all at the public good; the differences are only about the various modes of promoting it.

Common sense is something that everyone needs, few have, and none think they lack.

Content makes poor men rich; discontentment makes rich men poor.

Creditors have better memories than debtors.

Do not anticipate trouble, or worry about what may never happen. Keep in the sunlight.

Don't go to the doctor with every distemper, nor to the lawyer with every quarrel, nor to the pot for every thirst.

Don't misinform your Doctor nor your Lawyer.

Each year one vicious habit rooted out, in time might make the worst man good throughout.

Early to bed and early to rise, makes a man healthy, wealthy, and wise.

Eat to live, and not live to eat.

Eat to please yourself, but dress to please others.

Educate your children to self-control, to the habit of holding passion and prejudice and evil tendencies subject to an upright and reasoning will, and you have done much to abolish misery from their future and crimes from society.

Employ your time well, if you mean to get leisure.

Energy and persistence conquer all things.

Fear to do ill, and you need fear naught else.

Glass, china, and reputation are easily cracked and never well mended.

God heals, and the Doctor takes the Fees.

God helps them who help themselves.

Happiness consists more in small conveniences or pleasures that occur every day, than in great pieces of good fortune that happen but seldom to a man in the course of his life.

Having been poor is no shame, being ashamed of it is.

Having lived long, I have experienced many instances of being obliged by better information or fuller consideration to change opinions, even on important subjects, which I once thought right, but found to be otherwise.

He that falls in love with himself, will have no Rivals.

He that is known to pay punctually and exactly to the time he promises, may at any time, and on any occasion, raise all the money his friends can spare.

He that is of the opinion money will do everything may well be suspected of doing everything for money.

He who sacrifices freedom for security deserves neither.

He's the best physician that knows the worthlessness of the most medicines.

Hide not your talents, they for use were made. What's a sundial in the shade?

Hope and faith may be more firmly built upon charity, than charity upon faith and hope.

I don't believe in stereotypes. I prefer to hate people on a more personal basis.

I look upon death to be as necessary to our constitution as sleep.

I never knew a man who was good at making excuses who was good at anything else.

I never saw an oft-removed tree, nor yet an oft-removed family, that throve so well as those that settled be.

I would advise you to read with a pen in hand, and enter in a little book short hints of what you find that is curious, or that may be useful; for this will be the best method of imprinting such particulars in your memory.

If a man empties his purse into his head, no man can take it away from him. An investment in knowledge always pays the best interest.

If a man empties his purse into his head, no man can take it away from him. An investment in knowledge always pays the best interest.

If a sound body and a sound mind, which is as much as to say health and virtue, are to be preferred before all other considerations, ought not men, in choosing a business either for themselves or children, to refuse such as are unwholesome for the body, and such as make a man too dependent, too much obliged to please others, and too much subjected to their humors in order to be recommended and get a livelihood?

If you are active and prosperous, or young, or in good health, it may be easier for you to augment your means than to diminish your wants. But if you are wise, you will do both at the same time, young or old, rich or poor, sick or well; and if you are wise, you will do both in such a way as to augment the general happiness of society.

If you know how to spend less than you get, you have the philosopher's stone.

If you would know the value of money, go try to borrow some; for he that goes a-borrowing goes a-sorrowing.

If you would not be forgotten, as soon as you are dead and rotten, either write things worth reading, or do things worth the writing.

If you would persuade, you must appeal to interest rather than intellect.

In this world nothing can be said to be certain, except death and taxes.

It is a common error in friends, when they would extol their friends, to make comparisons, and to depreciate the merits of others.

It is the working man who is the happy man. It is the idle man who is the miserable man.

It seems to me, that if statesmen had a little more arithmetic, or were accustomed to calculation, wars would be much less frequent.

Life, like a dramatic piece, should not only be conducted with regularity, but it should finish handsomely.

Life's tragedy is that we get old too soon and wise too late.

Lost time is never found again.

Man and woman have each of them qualities and tempers in which the other is deficient, and which in union contribute to the common felicity.

Men are subject to various inconveniences merely through lack of a small share of courage, which is a quality very necessary in the common occurrences of life, as well as in a battle. How many impertinences do we daily suffer with great uneasiness, because we have not courage enough to discover our dislike.

Most men die from the neck up at age twenty-five because they stop dreaming.

Necessity never made a good bargain.

No nation was ever ruined by trade.

One today is worth two tomorrows.

Our opinions are not in our own power; they are formed and governed much by circumstances that are often as inexplicable as they are irresistible.

Rather go to bed without dinner than to rise in debt.

Reading makes a full man, meditation a profound man, discourse a clear man.

Security without liberty is called prison.

Some, to make themselves considerable, pursue learning; others grasp at wealth; some aim at being thought witty; and others are only careful to make the most of a handsome person; but what is wit, or wealth, or form, or learning, when compared with virtue? It is true we love the handsome, we applaud the learned, and we fear the rich and powerful; but we even worship and adore the virtuous.

Speak ill of no man, but speak all the good you know of everybody.

The ancients tell us what is best; but we must learn of the moderns what is fittest.

The art of getting riches consists very much in thrift. All men are not equally qualified for getting money, but it is in the power of every one alike to practice this virtue.

The best of all medicines are rest and fasting.

The best thing to give to your enemy is forgiveness; to an opponent, tolerance; to a friend, your heart; to your child, a good example; to a father, deference; to your mother, conduct that will make her proud of you; to yourself, respect; to all others, charity.

The Constitution only gives people the right to pursue happiness. You have to catch it yourself.

The eye of the master will do more work than both his hands.

The most trifling actions of a man, in my opinion, as well as the smallest features and lineaments of the face give a nice observer some notion of his mind.

The way to be safe, is never to be secure.

The way to secure peace is to be prepared for war. They that are on their guard, and appear ready to receive their adversaries, are in much less danger of being attacked, than the supine, secure, and negligent.

The wit of conversation consists more in finding it in others, than showing a great deal yourself. He who goes out of your company pleased with his own facetiousness and ingenuity, will the sooner come into it again.

The worship of God is a duty; the hearing and reading of sermons may be useful; but if men rest in hearing and praying, as too many do, it is as if a tree should value itself in being watered and putting forth leaves, though it never produced any fruit.

There are in life real evils enough, and it is folly to afflict ourselves with imaginary ones; it is time enough when the real ones arrive.

There are three things extremely hard: steel, a diamond, and to know one's self.

There are two ways of being happy — we may either diminish our wants or augment our means — either will do, the result is the same; and it is for each man to decide for himself, and do that which happens to be the easiest. If you are idle or sick or poor, however hard it may be to diminish your wants, it will be harder to augment your means.

There is much difference between imitating a man and counterfeiting him.

Those that won't be counseled can't be helped.

To be content, look backward on those who possess less than yourself, not forward on those who possess more. If this does not make you content, you don't deserve to be happy.

To expect people to be good, to be just, to be temperate, etc., without showing them how they should become so, seems like the ineffectual charity mentioned by the apostle, which consisted in saying to the hungry, the cold and the naked, be ye fed, be ye warmed, be ye clothed, without showing them how they should get food, fire or clothing.

To lengthen thy Life, lessen thy Meals.

To succeed, jump as quickly at opportunities as you do at conclusions.

To the generous mind the heaviest debt is that of gratitude, when it is not in our power to repay it.

Tricks and treachery are the practice of fools, that don't have brains enough to be honest.

We are all born ignorant, but one must work hard to remain stupid.

We need a revolution every 200 years, because all governments become stale and corrupt after 200 years.

We shall rise refreshed in the morning.

Well done is better than well said.

When I am employed in serving others, I do not look upon myself as conferring favors, but as paying debts. I have received much kindness from men to whom I shall never have an opportunity of making the least direct returns; and numberless mercies from God, who is infinitely above being benefited by our services. Those kindnesses from men I can, therefore, only return on their fellow-men, and I can only show my gratitude for those mercies from God by a readiness to help His other children.

When the well's dry, we know the worth of water.

When there is so much to be done for yourself, your family, and your country, be up by peep of day! Let not the sun look down and say, 'Inglorious here he lies!'

When you incline to have new clothes, look first well over the old ones, and see if you cannot shift with them another year, either by scouring, mending, or even patching if necessary. Remember, a patch on your coat, and money in your pocket, is better and more creditable, than a writ on your back, and no money to take it off.

When you're finished changing, you're finished.

Where liberty is, there is my country.

Wink at small faults; remember thou hast great ones.

Without continual growth and progress, such words as improvement, achievement, and success have no meaning.

Words may show a man's wit but actions his meaning.

Work as if you were to live a hundred years. Pray as if you were to die tomorrow.

Would you live with ease, do what you ought and not what you please.

You may delay, but time will not.

www.ingramcontent.com/pod-product-compliance
Lightning Source LLC
Chambersburg PA
CBHW071256070526
44583CB00017B/2501